VERTICAL BELLEVUE

marques vickers

VERTICAL BELLEVUE
Architecture Above A Boomburb Skyline

MARQUIS PUBLISHING
HERRON ISLAND, WASHINGTON

TABLE OF CONTENTS

Symetra Building, 777 108th Avenue NE
Ten20 Plaza, 10710 NE 10th Street

The Bravern Complex, 11111 NE 8th Street
One Lincoln Tower, Westin Hotel, 600 Bellevue Way NE

SOMA Towers, 288 106th Avenue NE

Bellevue Pacific Center, 118 106th Avenue NE

Civica Building. 225 108th Avenue NE

Columbia West, 155 108th Avenue NE

Park88 Building, 88 102nd Avenue NE

AC Marriott Hotel, 200 110th Avenue NE

Brio Apartments, 1021 112th Avenue NE

Eight Eighty-Eight Tower, 888 108th Avenue NE

Paccar Building, 777 106th Avenue NE

One 88 Condominiums, 200 105th Avenue NE

ABOUT THE AUTHOR

Edition 1

Published by Marquis Publishing
Herron Island, Washington USA

Vickers, Marques, 1957

VERTICAL BELLEVUE: Architecture Above A Boomburb Skyline

Dedicated to my Daughters Charline and Caroline.

The Glass Curtain Architecture of Bellevue Washington

Straddling Lake Washington and connected to urban Seattle by two floating bridges, Bellevue is considered an Eastside *boomburb* (booming suburb). The contemporary city features a clustered downtown concentration of high-rise glass skinned office and commercial structures. Bellevue, which translates into *beautiful view* in French, is a 37-square mile community with a population of 144,000. The cornerstone development is the Bellevue Square shopping center. Enlargement has expanded significantly beginning with the 1990s technology industry expansion.

The distinction between skyscrapers and multi-level constructions remains based on height. The term *skyscraper* refers to buildings exceeding 40 stories and 500 feet (150+ meters). Prominent skyscrapers have been described as pillars that connect earth to the heavens.

Bellevue's current trajectory and ambitions are more modestly scaled.

The origin of high-rise constructions date back to ancient Rome. Living spaces sometimes reached the equivalent of ten story structures, approximately 80 feet (25 meters). The lower floors generally accommodated merchants, shops and wealthy families. The upper floors were reserved for the lower classes, principally due to the inconveniences of mounting staircases on foot.

During the Medieval era, urban centers often featured larger numbers of high-rise constructions predominantly for defense and demonstrations of wealth. The most distinctive rose up to 300 feet (90 meters). 17th century Edinburgh was a renowned example of coordinated and advanced functional high-rise buildings.

With the invention of the elevator in the mid-19th century, multi-storied residential and commercial applications became more prevalent and practical. Building elevations rose towards the conclusion of the century.

A fundamental shift in structural emphasis began. Masonry based walls supporting the weight of structures were replaced by steel spined framing. The load-bearing hollow cylinders supported wall curtains. They proved more resistant to lateral factors such as strong prevailing winds and earthquakes. This construction technique more evenly distributed weight and better accommodated the heavy forces of gravity.

During the 20th century, high-rise constructions were designed even more slender. This innovation enabled less wind exposure and theoretically transmitted more interior daylight. Wind has proven a more poignant stress factor than seismic concerns. A catastrophic earthquake may radically alter that perception one day.

Wind speeds increase proportionately based on their distance from the ground. Energy consumption costs rise for the higher exposed floor levels creating insulation and CO_2 emissions challenges. Glass reflects a significant portion of sunlight, keeping building interiors cooler, often minimizing exorbitant air-conditioning costs. Tinting enables adequate filtered lighting for adjacent window areas, but often leaves core interior spaces darker resulting in higher lighting demands.

Despite the attractiveness of reflective glass panes, their widespread prevalence has cultivated critics within the design industry. Many outspoken detractors have dismissed them as monotonous and archaic. Their criticism is directed pointedly towards some of the undesirable realities imposed by reflective glass as an exterior skin.

The traditional considerations for employing glass have included economics, ease and speed of installation and weight factors. Glass is one-twelfth the weight of brick. Unlike masonry, maintenance may ultimately prove the most imposing challenge. Many early styles of paneling are only guaranteed with 25-year lifespans.

Falling and detached panes, particularly amidst natural disasters pose ongoing threats. Ample research and precedent data for evaluation is often lacking but will influence the level of future usage advisability.

The expense for replacement of fatigued panels can be exorbitant. International urban centers such as Shanghai have placed moratoriums for new constructions intending to employ reflective glass skins. Added to that, privacy issues due to the visibility of window exposure and heat and light reflection onto other properties have raised concerns and scrutiny.

Aesthetically, glass by its inherent nature poses unique display dilemmas. Pillowing is an effect where separate glass panels appear warped or even *pillow-like* instead of smooth and uniform. Glimmering is another effect of mirrored glass projecting twisted light shapes and images.

Proponents of glass-sheathed walls cite fresh innovations in glass composition featuring less tinting will minimize concerns. Many architects are downsizing the spatial surface areas employed in exterior design. They are integrating smaller components of glass into mixed-use combinations of stone, brick and metals.

Economics, engineering and construction management remain essential elements to preserving an equilibrium between beauty and practicality. Significantly sized glass curtains may ultimately be de-emphasized with shifting building design preferences, particularly in moderately scaled suburban backdrops.

In Bellevue, the sleek and gleaming reflective glass curtains still reign. The future and composition of Bellevue's skyline will undoubtedly mirror the fortunes and ambitions of advanced high technology.

909 ELEMENTS PLAZA,
909 112TH AVENUE NE

909 ELEMENTS PLAZA,
909 112TH AVENUE NE

909 Elements Plaza,
909 112th Avenue NE

909 ELEMENTS PLAZA,
909 112TH AVENUE NE

14

958 Elements Plaza
958 111th Avenue NE

958 ELEMENTS PLAZA
958 111TH AVENUE NE

958 ELEMENTS PLAZA
958 111TH AVENUE NE

958 ELEMENTS PLAZA
958 111TH AVENUE NE

958 ELEMENTS PLAZA
958 111TH AVENUE NE

989 ELEMENTS PLAZA
989 112TH AVENUE NE

989 ELEMENTS PLAZA
989 112TH AVENUE NE

989 Elements Plaza
989 112th Avenue NE

989 Elements Plaza
989 112th Avenue NE

PLAZA EAST BUILDING
11100 EIGHTH AVENUE NE

PLAZA EAST BUILDING
11100 EIGHTH AVENUE NE

BELLEVUE CORPORATE BUILDING
600 108TH STREET

BELLEVUE CORPORATE BUILDING
600 108TH STREET

BELLEVUE CORPORATE BUILDING
600 108TH STREET

NINE TWO NINE TOWER
929 108TH STREET

NINE TWO NINE TOWER
929 108TH STREET

NINE TWO NINE TOWER
929 108TH STREET

ONE TWELFTH AT TWELFTH BUILDING
1100-1200 112TH AVENUE NE

ONE TWELFTH AT TWELFTH BUILDING
1100-1200 112TH AVENUE NE

ONE TWELFTH AT TWELFTH BUILDING
1100-1200 112TH AVENUE NE

ONE TWELFTH AT TWELFTH BUILDING
1100-1200 112TH AVENUE NE

WASHINGTON SQUARE CONDOS
10600-10650 NE 9TH PLACE

WASHINGTON SQUARE CONDOS
10600-10650 NE 9TH PLACE

WASHINGTON SQUARE CONDOS
10600-10650 NE 9TH PLACE

WASHINGTON SQUARE CONDOS
10600-10650 NE 9TH PLACE

WASHINGTON SQUARE CONDOS
10600-10650 NE 9TH PLACE

ASHTON BELLEVUE
10710 NE 10TH STREET

ASHTON BELLEVUE
10710 NE 10TH STREET

ASHTON BELLEVUE
10710 NE 10TH STREET

AVALON TOWERS
10349 NE 10TH STREET

AVALON TOWERS
10349 NE 10TH STREET

BELLEVUE PLACE
10500 NE 8TH STREET

BELLEVUE PLACE
10500 NE 8TH STREET

BELLEVUE TOWER COMPLEX
106TH AVENUE NE

BELLEVUE TOWER COMPLEX
106TH AVENUE NE

BELLEVUE TOWER COMPLEX
106TH AVENUE NE

BELLEVUE TOWER COMPLEX
106TH AVENUE NE

BELLEVUE TOWER COMPLEX
106TH AVENUE NE

BELLEVUE TOWER COMPLEX
106TH AVENUE NE

BELLEVUE TOWER COMPLEX
106TH AVENUE NE

BELLEVUE TOWER COMPLEX
106TH AVENUE NE

BELLEVUE TOWER COMPLEX
106TH AVENUE NE

BELLEVUE TOWER COMPLEX
106TH AVENUE NE

BELLEVUE TOWER COMPLEX
106TH AVENUE NE

CENTER 425
415 106TH AVENUE NE (2016)

CENTER 425
415 106TH AVENUE NE (2016)

CENTER 425
415 106TH AVENUE NE (2016)

Center425, 415 106th Avenue NE

Center425, 415 106th Avenue NE

Center425, 415 106th Avenue NE

CITY CENTRE BELLEVUE
500 108TH AVENUE NE

CITY CENTRE BELLEVUE
500 108TH AVENUE NE

CITY CENTRE BELLEVUE
500 108TH AVENUE NE

CITY CENTRE BELLEVUE
500 108TH AVENUE NE

CITY CENTRE BELLEVUE
500 108TH AVENUE NE

CITY CENTRE BELLEVUE
500 108TH AVENUE NE

CITY CENTRE PLAZA
555 110TH AVENUE NE

CITY CENTRE BELLEVUE
500 108TH AVENUE NE

CITY CENTRE BELLEVUE
500 108TH AVENUE NE

CITY CENTRE BELLEVUE
500 108TH AVENUE NE

CITY CENTRE BELLEVUE
500 108TH AVENUE NE

EXPEDIA BUILDING
333 108TH AVENUE NE

EXPEDIA BUILDING
333 108TH AVENUE NE

EXPEDIA BUILDING
333 108TH AVENUE NE

HYATT REGENCY HOTEL
900 BELLEVUE WAY NE

HYATT REGENCY HOTEL
900 BELLEVUE WAY NE

HYATT REGENCY HOTEL
900 BELLEVUE WAY NE

KEY CENTER BUILDING
601 108TH AVENUE NE

KEY CENTER BUILDING
601 108TH AVENUE NE

KEY CENTER BUILDING
601 108TH AVENUE NE

LINCOLN SQUARE
110 BELLEVUE WAY NE

LINCOLN SQUARE
110 BELLEVUE WAY NE

LINCOLN SQUARE
110 BELLEVUE WAY NE

LINCOLN SQUARE
110 BELLEVUE WAY NE

LINCOLN SQUARE EXTENSION
410 BELLEVUE WAY NE (2016)

LINCOLN SQUARE EXTENSION
410 BELLEVUE WAY NE (2016)

LINCOLN SQUARE EXTENSION
410 BELLEVUE WAY NE (2016)

LINCOLN SQUARE EXTENSION
410 BELLEVUE WAY NE (2016)

LINCOLN SQUARE EXTENSION
410 BELLEVUE WAY NE (2016)

Lincoln Square Addition, 10400 NE 4th Street

Lincoln Square Addition, 10400 NE 4th Street

Lincoln Square Addition, 10400 NE 4th Street

ONE BELLEVUE CENTER
411 108TH AVENUE NE

ONE BELLEVUE CENTER
411 108TH AVENUE NE

Puget Sound Energy
355 110th Avenue NE

PUGET SOUND ENERGY
355 110TH AVENUE NE

PUGET SOUND ENERGY
355 110TH AVENUE NE

PUGET SOUND ENERGY EAST BUILDING
355 110TH AVENUE NE

PUGET SOUND ENERGY
355 110TH AVENUE NE

Skyline Building
10900 NE Fourth Avenue

Skyline Building
10900 NE Fourth Avenue

Skyline Building
10900 NE 4th Street

Skyline Building
10900 NE 4th Street

SYMETRA BUILDING
777 108TH AVENUE NE

Symetra Building
777 108th Avenue NE

Symetra Building
777 108th Avenue NE

SYMETRA BUILDING
777 108TH AVENUE NE

TEN20 PLAZA
10710 NE 10TH STREET

Ten20 Plaza
10710 NE 10th Street

TEN20 PLAZA
10710 NE 10TH STREET

THE BAVERN COMPLEX
11111 NE 8TH STREET

THE BAVERN COMPLEX
11111 NE 8TH STREET

THE BAVERN COMPLEX
11111 NE 8TH STREET

THE BAVERN COMPLEX
11111 NE 8TH STREET

THE BAVERN COMPLEX
11111 NE 8TH STREET

One Lincoln Tower/Westin Hotel
600 Bellevue Way NE

ONE LINCOLN TOWER/WESTIN HOTEL
600 BELLEVUE WAY NE

ONE LINCOLN TOWER/WESTIN HOTEL
600 BELLEVUE WAY NE

ONE LINCOLN TOWER/WESTIN HOTEL
600 BELLEVUE WAY NE

SOMA Towers, 288 106th Avenue NE (2016)

SOMA Towers, 288 106th Avenue NE (2016)

SOMA Towers, 288 106th Avenue NE (2016)

SOMA Towers, 288 106th Avenue NE (2016)

SOMA Towers, 288 106th Avenue NE (2016)

SOMA Towers, 288 106th Avenue NE (2016)

SOMA Towers, 288 106th Avenue NE (2016)

SOMA Towers, 288 106th Avenue NE

SOMA Towers, 288 106th Avenue NE

SOMA Towers, 288 106th Avenue NE

SOMA Towers, 288 106th Avenue NE

SOMA Towers, 288 106th Avenue NE

BELLEVUE PACIFIC CENTER
118 106TH AVENUE NE

BELLEVUE PACIFIC CENTER
118 106TH AVENUE NE

CIVICA BUILDING
225 108TH AVENUE NE

CIVICA BUILDING
225 108TH AVENUE NE

CIVICA BUILDING
225 108TH AVENUE NE

Columbia Building, 155 108th Avenue NE

Park88 Building
88 102nd Avenue NE

PARK88 BUILDING
88 102ND AVENUE NE

Marriott Hotel, 200 110th Avenue NE

Marriott Hotel, 200 110th Avenue NE

Brio Apartments, 1021 112th Avenue NE

Brio Apartments, 1021 112th Avenue NE

Brio Apartments, 1021 112th Avenue NE

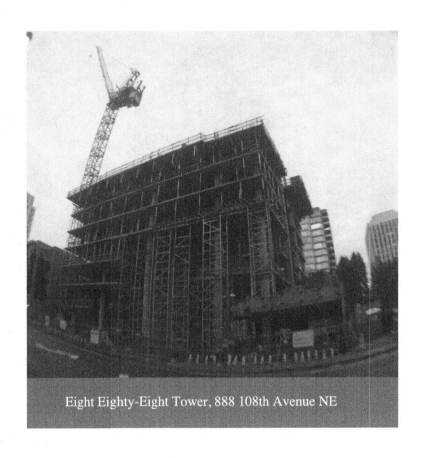

Eight Eighty-Eight Tower, 888 108th Avenue NE

Eight Eighty-Eight Tower, 888 108th Avenue NE

Paccar Building, 777 106th Avenue NE

Paccar Building, 777 106th Avenue NE

One 88 Condominiums, 200 105th Avenue NE

One 88 Condominiums, 200 105th Avenue NE

Author and Photographer Marques Vickers was born in 1957 in Vallejo, California. He graduated from Azusa Pacific University in Los Angeles and became the Director of the Burbank Chamber of Commerce between 1979-84.

Professionally, he has operated travel, apparel, and publishing businesses. His paintings and sculptures have been exhibited in art galleries and museums in the United States and Europe. He has previously lived in the Burgundy and Languedoc regions of France and currently lives on Herron Island in western Washington.

He has written and published over seventy books on a variety of subjects including the art and auction industry, architecture, wine, travel, crime, social satire and fiction.

Made in the USA
Coppell, TX
01 December 2020

42600491R10085